The Technology of Farming

Producing Dairy and Eggs

Jane Bingham

www.raintreepublishers.co.uk
Visit our website to find out more information about Raintree books.

To order:
☎ Phone 0845 6044371
🖹 Fax +44 (0) 1865 312263
✉ Email myorders@raintreepublishers.co.uk

Customers from outside the UK please telephone +44 1865 312262

Raintree is an imprint of Capstone Global Library Limited, a company incorporated in England and Wales having its registered office at 7 Pilgrim Street, London, EC4V 6LB – Registered company number: 6695582

Text © Capstone Global Library Limited 2013
First published in hardback in 2013
The moral rights of the proprietor have been asserted.

Edited by Abby Colich, Megan Cotugno, and Nancy Dickmann
Designed by Victoria Allen
Picture research by Elizabeth Alexander
Illustrations by Oxford Designers & Illustrators
Originated by Capstone Global Library Ltd
Printed and bound in China by China Translation and Printing Services Ltd

ISBN 978 1 406 24049 8
16 15 14 13 12
10 9 8 7 6 5 4 3 2 1

British Library Cataloguing in Publication Data
Bingham, Jane.
  Producing dairy and eggs. -- (The technology of farming)
  1. Dairy farming--Juvenile literature. 2. Eggs--Production--Juvenile literature. 3. Agricultural innovations--Juvenile literature.
  I. Title II. Series
  636.2'142-dc23
A full catalogue record for this book is available from the British Library.

Acknowledgements
The author and publisher are grateful to the following for permission to reproduce copyright material: Alamy: pp. 17 (©North Wind Picture Archives), 19 (©Danita Delimont), 32 (©Peter Horree), 33 (©Paris Market), 37 (©Tim Scrivener), 43 (© Nick Turner); Corbis: pp. 7 (© Wu Hong/epa), 35 (© Layne Kennedy); Getty Images: pp. 9 (Dagli Orti), 11 (Jean-Francois Millet/The Bridgeman Art Library), 13 (Wallace Kirkland/Time Life Pictures), 14 (Lewis W. Hine/George Eastman House), 15 (Universal History Archive), 25 (Chien-min Chung), 31 (Bloomberg News/Chris Warde-Jones); Photolibrary: pp. 18, 20, 34, 41; Shutterstock: pp. 4 (© gillmar), 6 (© Nadezhda Bolotina), 27 (© oznuroz), 30 (© Magone), 39 (© Igumnova Irina), 40 (© Sveta San).

Cover photo of milking of cows in a modern milking plant reproduced with permission from Photolibrary (CNS CNS/Sinopictures).

Every effort has been made to contact copyright holders of material reproduced in this book. Any omissions will be rectified in subsequent printings if notice is given to the publisher.

Disclaimer
All the internet addresses (URLs) given in this book were valid at the time of going to press. However, due to the dynamic nature of the internet, some addresses may have changed, or sites may have changed or ceased to exist since publication. While the author and Publishers regret any inconvenience this may cause readers, no responsibility for any such changes can be accepted by either the author or the Publishers.

Contents

Some words appear in the text in bold, **like this**. You can find out what they mean by looking in the glossary.

How are dairy and eggs produced?

The word "dairy" is used to describe milk and other foods made from milk. Cream, butter, cheese, and yoghurt are all **dairy products**. Most of the dairy products that we eat and drink come from cows.

The average dairy cow produces around 22 to 26 litres (6 or 7 gallons) of milk per day. That is about 100 glasses of milk!

From the cow to you

Most dairy farmers in **developed countries** rely on **technology**. They use machines to milk their cows, and the milk is collected in a tanker, which is a lorry with a very large refrigerated tank. The tanker transports the milk to a special factory known as a dairy **plant**.

At the dairy plant, the milk is **processed** to make sure it is safe to drink. Then it is poured into cartons, bottles, or other containers. The full milk containers are packed into refrigerated lorries, which carry them to shops and supermarkets. In some places, milk is delivered directly to people's homes.

Modern technology

Dairy plants today use the latest technology to produce a range of dairy foods. This book will describe the methods and machines used in modern dairy plants. You can also find out how dairy foods were produced in the past.

Traditional methods

Some farmers in developing countries use very little technology. They milk their animals by hand, and they produce cheese and other products with the help of very simple tools and machines. These farmers use traditional methods that have been practised for thousands of years.

Not just cows

Dairy products do not always come from cows. Many people enjoy goat's cheese. In Italy, mozzarella cheese is made from buffalo milk. In Greece feta cheese is usually made from sheep milk. In some parts of the world, people drink milk from yaks and camels and make cheese and yoghurt from it.

Eggs as well

This book discusses eggs as well as dairy products. Most of the eggs we eat are laid by hens (female chickens), but some people like to eat the eggs of geese, ducks, or quail. In parts of Africa, people eat guinea fowl eggs.

For many farmers today, egg production is big business. In some developed countries, egg producers keep many millions of hens. Eggs are usually processed and packed in an egg processing plant.

People of the Ural Mountains drink reindeer milk!

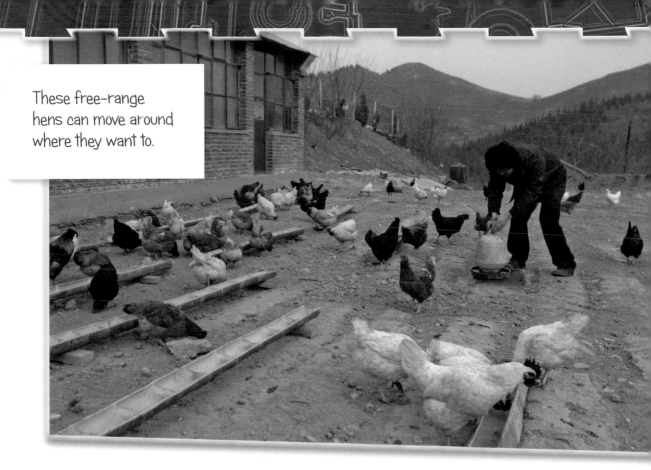

These free-range hens can move around where they want to.

Intensive or organic?

All modern farmers use technology, but some farmers use **intensive farming** methods in order to make their animals produce as much as possible. Most intensive farmers run large-scale farms, with a lot of machinery. They often feed their animals specially prepared food to make them more **productive**. Intensive farmers produce large quantities of food, but some people think that this type of farming can have a bad effect on the animals.

Other farmers take a different approach. They believe that cows and hens should only eat natural food and should not be given certain medicines when they are ill. They also make sure their animals have plenty of freedom to **roam** outside. This method of farming is sometimes known as **organic farming**. You can find out more about intensive and organic farming in this book.

How did dairy farming begin?

People have been milking animals for at least 10,000 years. Around 8000 BC groups of nomads (wandering people) in central Asia began keeping herds of sheep and goats. These animals produced milk as well as providing wool, meat, and skins. At about the same time, farmers in the Middle East began to tame wild cattle. At first, the cattle were mainly used as working animals, but around 3000 BC Arab farmers started to keep dairy herds.

Learning to make cheese

Nobody knows when people first began making cheese, but there is an ancient legend that an Arab shepherd was the first cheese-maker. According to the legend, the shepherd was carrying milk in a sheep's stomach when he discovered that the milk had turned into solid cheese. A substance called **rennet**, which is found in the stomachs of all animals, had **reacted** with the milk to form cheese.

Ancient dairy farmers

The ancient Sumerians farmed in the Middle East from around 5000 to 2000 BC. They kept cows and goats for their milk and cheese and stored their cheese in tall pottery jars. The ancient Egyptians were also expert cheese-makers. In ancient Egypt, dairy products were mainly enjoyed by the wealthy.

This ancient Egyptian tomb painting shows a farmer milking a dairy cow. It dates from around 2000 BC.

Greeks and Romans

Farmers in ancient Greece kept sheep and goats for their milk and cheese. They made soft cheeses, like the feta cheese that is still made in Greece today. The Romans made soft cheeses, too, but they also developed a way of making hard cheeses.

The Romans practised their cheese-making skills in many parts of their empire. During the Roman period, farmers in France and Britain became very skilled at making cheese.

Family cows

In the Middle Ages (around AD 1000 to 1450), people all over Europe kept dairy cows. Families often had their own cow to supply all their milk, butter, and cheese. The cow was milked by the women and children of the family.

This illustration shows how a butter churn from the Middle Ages worked.

Handle is pushed up and down

Cream

Plunger with holes

Making butter at home

The woman of the house made the family's butter. First she skimmed off the cream that rose to the top of the milk. Then she used a wooden butter churn to turn the cream into butter. Simple butter churns are still used today in some parts of the world.

Early butter churn

For many centuries, people used a simple wooden churn to turn cream into butter. Cream was poured into a tall wooden barrel. Then a wooden plunger was pushed up and down inside the barrel to churn up the cream. The repeated movement of the plunger turned the liquid cream into solid butter.

Churning cream into butter was very hard work!

Dairy herds

By the 1700s, many towns and cities had grown throughout Europe, America, and Australia. People living in towns went to their local market to buy **dairy products**. Farmers in the country kept dairy herds, and their milk, cream, and cheese were taken to market by cart.

Parlours and dairies

Cows on farms were usually milked by women who were known as dairymaids or milkmaids. Milking took place in a building called a **milking parlour** (or a milking shed). Cream, butter, and cheese were produced in a cool room close to the milking parlour. This room was known as the dairy.

Gustaf de Laval (1845–1913)

The Swedish inventor Gustaf de Laval spent most of his life making improvements in dairy farming. In 1894, he designed a cream separator that made the job of separating cream from milk much easier and faster than before. The Laval separator was used all over the world.

Dairy breeds

Farmers kept special dairy cows that produced high-quality milk. Dairy breeds included Holsteins from the Netherlands, Ayrshires from Scotland, Brown Swiss from Switzerland, and Guernseys and Jerseys from the Channel Islands. When settlers arrived in North America, Australia, and New Zealand, they brought their dairy cows with them. The same basic breeds are kept in dairy farms all over the world.

The Laval separator worked by spinning milk very fast. The milk, which is heavier, was pulled outward against the walls of the separator. The cream, which is lighter, was collected in the middle. Then the cream and milk flowed out of separate spouts.

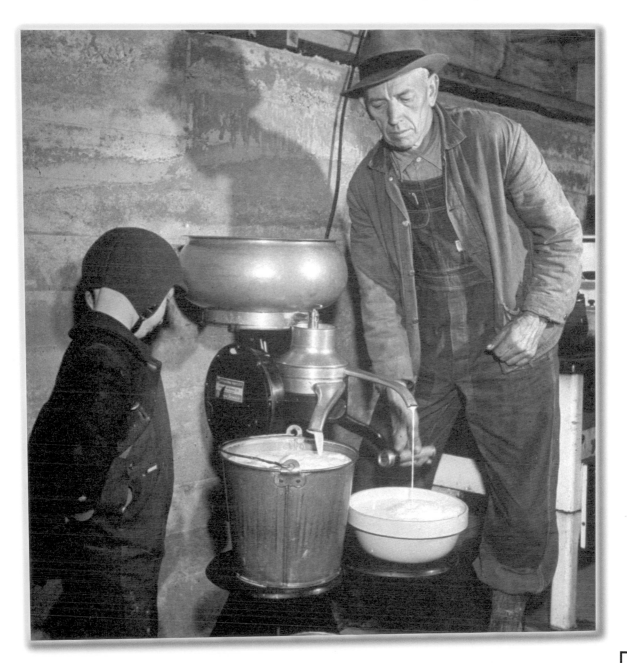

How did dairy farms develop?

By the 1850s, some farmers in Europe and the United States had started to **specialize** in dairy production. Instead of running a mixed farm with crops and animals, they had dairy farms with large herds of cows. But dairy farmers had to cope with some difficult challenges.

Dairy problems

Farmers with large herds faced the problem of storing large quantities of milk. Milk quickly turned sour, especially in hot weather. There was also the danger that milk could contain harmful **bacteria** (germs). People could catch diseases such as tuberculosis (a very serious lung disease) by drinking the milk of unhealthy cows.

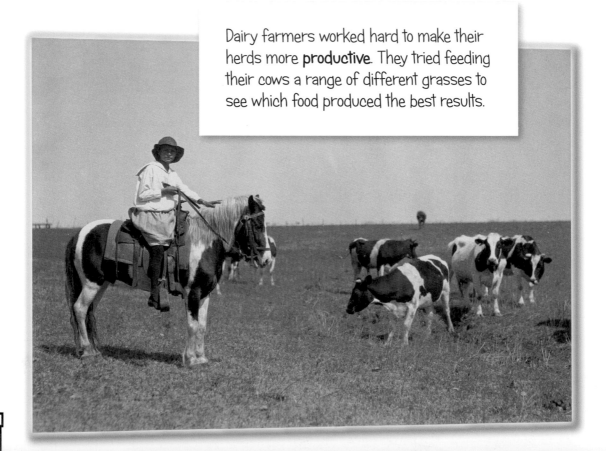

Dairy farmers worked hard to make their herds more **productive**. They tried feeding their cows a range of different grasses to see which food produced the best results.

Pasteurization

In 1862, Louis Pasteur discovered a method of treating milk by heating it and then cooling it quickly. This process was later called **pasteurization**. It makes milk last longer without turning sour and also makes it healthier to drink (see box). Pasteurization machines were first introduced in 1895. Almost all the milk that we buy today has been pasteurized. Unpasteurized milk is used to make some cheeses.

Louis Pasteur (1822–1895)

Louis Pasteur was a leading French chemist. He was one of the first scientists to recognize that all substances contain bacteria (germs). Pasteur realized that the bacteria in milk multiply very fast, causing milk to go "bad". He also discovered that most of these bacteria were destroyed when he heated milk. Heating milk also destroys many of the harmful germs that can cause illness. Pasteur's work saved many lives.

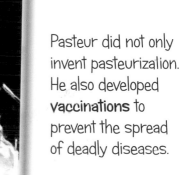

Pasteur did not only invent pasteurization. He also developed **vaccinations** to prevent the spread of deadly diseases.

Keeping cool

The process of pasteurization made milk last longer, but farmers still had the problem of keeping milk cold. This problem was not fully solved until the 1930s, when refrigerated tanks were introduced on farms.

Milking problems

As dairy farms grew in size, farmers struggled to milk all their cows. Cows had to be milked twice a day, and even experienced dairymaids could not milk more than six cows an hour. In the 19th century, many people tried to create a milking machine that copied the actions of the dairymaids. However, it was not until the 1920s that a really successful machine was invented.

The Mehring Milker

The Mehring Milker was first sold in 1891. It was the most popular of the early milking machines. It had four rubber cups that were fitted on to the cow's teats. The cups were attached to a pump that squeezed the cups regularly, and this action made the cow produce her milk.

Dairy plants

By the 1940s, most dairy farmers had stopped making their own butter and cheese. Instead, they sent their milk to a dairy **plant**, where the milk was treated and **processed** into other **dairy products**. The introduction of refrigerated tankers in the 1950s meant that ice-cold milk could be delivered directly from the farm to the dairy plant.

Traditional milking parlours, such as this one in the 19th century, began to change once machinery was introduced.

How did egg production begin?

Egg production began about 9,000 years ago when wild fowl were first tamed in China. Around the same time, chickens were being bred in India. Over the next few thousand years, red jungle fowl from China and India were transported to many parts of Asia, Africa, and Europe. They are the ancestors of our modern egg-laying hens.

Which bird is best?

In ancient Egypt and China, people kept chickens, geese, and ducks for their eggs. The practice of keeping chickens began in Europe around 700 BC, although goose eggs were also common in medieval Europe. In North America, American Indians kept wild turkeys for their meat and eggs, but when the early settlers arrived in America they brought their own chickens from Europe. Gradually, chickens became the standard egg-laying bird all over the world.

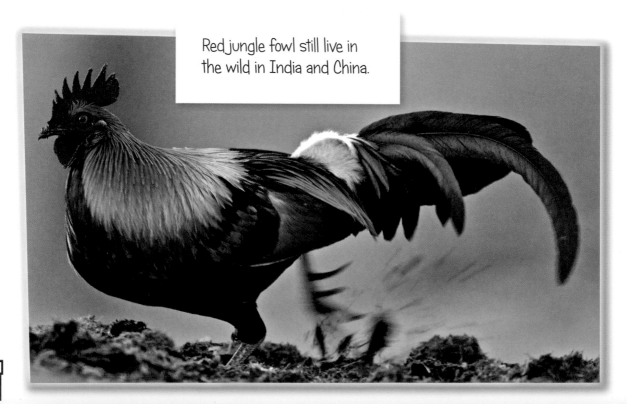

Red jungle fowl still live in the wild in India and China.

Over the centuries, people developed special breeds of chickens that were very good at laying eggs. The single-comb white leghorn is one of the most popular breeds.

Eggs for the family

By the 1200s, many families kept chickens of their own. The female hens lay an egg every day or every two days, so a family with several hens could collect some eggs every day. When the hens became too old to lay eggs, they were killed and eaten.

In **developed countries**, the practice of keeping family hens gradually died out. By the 1800s, most families were buying their eggs from farmers. However, in many parts of the world, families still keep a few hens to supply all the eggs they need.

Larger flocks

Until the 1900s, farmers kept a small flock of hens as part of a mixed farm. The hens slept in wooden hen houses (sometimes known as coops) and **roamed** freely during the day. By the 1920s, however, farmers were keeping much larger flocks. Their hens spent most of their time inside large hen houses.

The method of egg production where hens are kept in cages is known as **factory farming** or "battery farming". It has been widely criticized because it causes a lot of stress to hens.

Crowded hens

Hens in crowded hen houses experienced a range of problems. They became panicky and pecked at each other. They fought each other for food, and some of them starved. They also developed diseases from standing in their own droppings.

Hens in cages

In the 1930s, farmers began to keep hens in wire cages. The cages stood on shelves inside huge sheds. The hens fed from a food trough. Their eggs rolled into a metal chute, and their droppings fell through the floor of their cage.

Keeping hens in cages cut down on some diseases, but the birds were still very crowded. (There were usually five hens in each cage.) They still pecked at each other, and they became very stressed and unhealthy.

In the 1960s, egg producers realized that hens produced more eggs when they were kept in constant light. So the lights in the laying sheds were never turned off. Farmers also started "debeaking" their hens to stop them from pecking at each other. This involved burning off the sharp part of the hens' beaks.

What methods are used for milking?

Modern dairy farmers rely on milking machines. These machines make the job of milking much easier and faster than in the past. Today's farmers can milk between 100 and 220 cows per hour.

Milking machines

Modern milking machines have four teat cups made from stainless steel with a soft rubber lining. The cups are linked by a "claw" that leads into a tube for collecting milk. Each teat cup also has a small air tube leading into it. The air tube is linked to a pump that creates a regular squeezing and releasing movement. This movement makes the cow release her milk.

This diagram shows how teat cups collect milk.

Teat cup

Air tube leading to teat cup

Main air tube

Milk tube

Milk is collected here

Stage 1

Stage 2

Teat

Rubber lining

Milk

Air is pushed in

Air is sucked out

How does a milking machine work?

A milking machine works in two stages. In stage one, the pump pushes air through the air tube into the teat cup. The rubber lining expands and gently squeezes the teat, but no milk flows. In stage two, the pump sucks air out. The rubber lining collapses and releases the pressure on the teat. The teat relaxes and opens, and milk flows into the milk tube.

Rotary parlours

In the 1980s, the first rotary parlours were introduced. In a rotary parlour, the cows are loaded one at a time on to a circular platform that rotates very slowly. A dairy worker puts the cups on the cows as they move past. Then the milking machine does its work. By the time the platform has made a complete rotation, the cow has been milked. The cups are removed **automatically** and the cow's teats are sprayed with disinfectant. The cow steps off the platform and walks towards her feed.

Automatic milking systems

Over the last 30 years, some automatic milking systems (AMS) have been developed. In these systems, the cow decides when she wants to be milked. She walks towards an automatic gate, where a computer checks whether she has been recently milked. If the cow is allowed through the gate, she walks to a milking station (a place where she is milked). At the milking station, a **robotic arm** fits the milking machine on to the cow's teats. The cow is milked, the machine is removed, and the cow's teats are sprayed with disinfectant. All these processes are performed automatically.

Modern milking parlours

Modern **milking parlours** are designed to make milking as easy as possible. Cows enter the parlour through automatic gates, and dairy workers stand on sunken platforms so that they do not need to bend to reach the cows' teats.

Most rotary milking systems have places for around 40 cows. It is possible to milk up to 220 cows per hour using a rotary system.

How are milk and cream processed?

Milk and cream are usually **processed** at a dairy **plant** (factory). The first and most important process is **pasteurization**. This involves heating the milk to around 70°C (160°F) to make the milk last longer and to kill off harmful **bacteria**. Pasteurized milk can last up to three weeks if it is kept very cold.

UHT milk

Some milk is given a special heat treatment to make it last a very long time. This kind of milk is known as UHT milk, or long-life milk. (The initials UHT stand for ultra-heat-treated.) UHT milk is heated to 135°C (275°F) for a short time to kill germs. If it is kept in a sealed container, it can last for up to nine months without being refrigerated.

Powdered milk

Some milk has all the moisture removed from it in order to produce powdered milk. Powdered milk is an **ingredient** in many factory-made foods, such as cakes and biscuits. It is also used to make infant formula (milk for babies).

Cream and skimmed milk

Some of the milk in a dairy plant goes through a process to separate the cream from the milk. This is done in a large machine called a **centrifuge** (or spinner). After all the cream has been separated from the milk, a thin liquid called **skimmed milk** is left behind. People drink skimmed milk when they want to reduce the fat in their diet.

Giant centrifuges (spinners) are used to separate cream from milk in a dairy plant. They work in the same way as the cream separator described on page 13.

Homogenized milk

If cream is not removed from milk, it forms a thick layer on the milk's surface. In the past, people liked to have milk with cream on top. But now our milk is **homogenized**. This means the milk has gone through a process to spread the cream evenly throughout the milk (see page 29).

Semi-skimmed milk

Many people today like to drink semi-skimmed milk. To make semi-skimmed milk, a small proportion of cream is added back to skimmed milk. Then the cream is mixed up with the milk using the process of homogenization.

All sorts of cream

Cream is sold in a range of thicknesses, each with a different fat content. Clotted cream, a West Country speciality, has the highest fat content, at 55 per cent! Heavy double cream is about 48 per cent fat, and whipping cream is around 35 per cent. Single cream is a thinner cream with around 18 per cent fat. Whole milk is between 3 and 4 per cent fat. Ice cream is made by freezing cream slowly and adding a lot of sugar.

Unhomogenized milk
(milk with large
globules of cream)

Globules are
squeezed

Globules are
squeezed again

Homogenized milk
(milk with small
globules of cream)

How does a milk homogenizer work?

A milk homogenizer is a large metal container. Milk is poured into the homogenizer and forced at very high pressure through tiny spaces. This process breaks down the globules (drops) of cream in the milk and creates much smaller globules. The tiny globules of cream are no longer light enough to rise to the top of the milk, so they stay evenly spread throughout the milk.

How are other dairy foods produced?

Butter is one of the best-selling dairy foods. It is made by churning (stirring it vigorously) cream until it forms a solid mass (see page 11). In modern dairy **plants**, cream is churned in huge metal containers. Sometimes vegetable oil is mixed with the butter to make it soft and easy to spread.

Curds and whey

Many dairy products are made from **fermented** milk. This is milk that has gone sour. When milk is fermented, it separates into two substances: solid **curds** and liquid **whey**. The curds are turned into cheese. Whey is often fed to farm animals.

Cottage cheese is made up of curds and whey. The lumps are tiny cheese curds and the liquid is whey. It has a mild flavour because the bacteria in the curds have not been left to ferment for long.

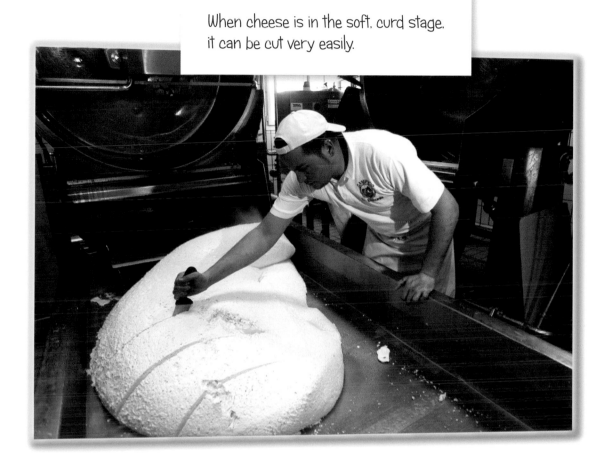

When cheese is in the soft, curd stage, it can be cut very easily.

Producing cheese

When milk is fermented to make cheese, a substance called **rennet** is added. This makes the curds more solid. The resulting cheese is soft and slightly rubbery. Some soft cheeses are finished at this stage.

Hard cheeses are heated to 35°C to 55°C (95°F to 131°F). The gentle heat removes more whey, but it does not destroy the **bacteria** in the cheese. The bacteria continue the fermenting process, creating a cheese with a strong, tangy flavour. Some cheeses are left to **mature** for a few weeks. Others take much longer. Parmesan cheese is matured for at least a year in order to gain its strong flavour.

All sorts of cheeses

There are hundreds of different cheeses, and they each have their own recipe. The makers of the Swiss cheese Emmental use special bacteria to ferment their curd. The bacteria produce large bubbles that leave holes in the cheese when it hardens. Dutch cheese-makers wash their curds in warm water to make them taste less tangy. This creates mild cheeses, such as Edam or Gouda.

Cheese presses have been used for thousands of years. This one dates back to the 1800s.

Cheese press

A cheese press is used to squeeze the last drops of moisture from a cheese. A heavy weight pushes down on the cheese, and liquid escapes through the bottom of the press.

While they are maturing, blue cheeses are pierced with needles to create tiny air holes. Air enters the cheese and helps the mould grow.

Mozzarella and blue cheese

The curd for mozzarella cheese is stretched and **kneaded** in hot water, rather like kneading dough to make bread. This makes the cheese stretchy and stringy when you cook it. Blue cheeses have a special mould added to them. As the mould develops, it turns a blue-green colour and adds a very strong flavour to the cheese.

Making yoghurt

Yoghurt is made from fermented milk that has been heated. First the milk is heated to around 80°C (176°F). This prevents the milk from forming curds and whey. Then the milk is cooled to around 45°C (113°F). The milk is kept warm for four to seven hours while it ferments and turns into yoghurt.

How are eggs processed?

Today's egg producers usually collect their eggs as soon as they are laid. The eggs are placed on trays and stored in a cool place. Some large egg farms have their own **processing plants**. Others send their eggs to a processing plant in refrigerated trucks. At the plant, the eggs are washed, checked, graded, and packed. Many of these processes are performed **automatically** by special machines.

Cleaning

When the eggs arrive at the plant, they are transferred to a **conveyor belt**. The belt carries the eggs through all the processing stages. The first stage is cleaning. The eggs are turned gently as brushes and water jets move carefully across them. Then a fan dries the eggs.

Rows of tiny suction cups gently lift up the eggs and place them on the conveyor belt. (The colour of the eggs – brown or white – depends on the breed of hen that laid them.)

The process of checking eggs is called candling. In the past, eggs were checked by holding each one in front of a candle.

Checking

After the eggs have been cleaned, the conveyor belt carries them into a **candling** room. This is a darkened area with bright lights shining under the eggs. An experienced checker spots any eggs that are old or cracked. Old eggs have a thinner albumen (or egg "white") than fresh eggs. This makes the yolk look darker when a light is shone through the egg. Checkers also look for any unusual spots that could be a sign of disease.

Grading

At the candling stage, eggs are given the grades A, B, or C. The A-grade eggs are the best quality. They are sold to supermarkets. B-grade eggs are healthy and uncracked, but they are oddly shaped so they cannot be sold in shops. They are sent to factories to be used in cakes, biscuits, and other foods. C-grade eggs are cracked or old and cannot be used for human food. They are sent to egg-breakers, who use their shells. Dried eggshells are used in animal feed and soil **fertilizers**.

Weighing

Once all the A-grade eggs have been selected, they are weighed by an **automatic** weighing machine. The machine sorts the eggs into different sizes according to their weight. In the United Kingdom, eggs can be extra large, large, medium, and small.

British Lion Organization

The British Lion Organization is responsible for checking the safety of British eggs. British Lion inspectors are sent to egg processing plants to check on all their processes. If a plant meets the correct standards of **hygiene** and food safety, then their eggs are given a stamp showing a red lion.

Packing

After the eggs have been weighed, a packing machine places the eggs in the correct carton for their weight. Eggs may be packed in cardboard or **polystyrene** cartons. Then the cartons are stacked in lorries, ready to be sent out to shops.

In the final stage of egg production. the eggs are packed into cartons. Throughout the production process. the eggs are never touched by human hands.

What methods do organic farmers use?

During the last 20 years, there has been a growing interest in **organic farming**. Organic farmers aim to produce foods that are as natural as possible. They feed their animals food that is free from chemicals and allow them to **roam** outside.

Intensive or organic?

Today's dairy farmers have to make a choice between **intensive farming** or organic farming. Many dairy farmers in Europe and the United States choose to use very intensive methods.

Intensive dairy farmers feed their cows **high-protein** cereals to increase their milk production. Cows on intensive farms in the United States are also given **growth hormones** to make them produce more milk, and **antibiotic** drugs to keep them free from diseases. (In other countries, cows are not given growth hormones.) A few intensive farmers practice **zero grazing**, which means keeping cows indoors for most of their lives. Some people believe that these practices have a bad effect on the cows' milk, but most people drink milk from cows that have been intensively farmed.

The Soil Association

The Soil Association supports organic farmers and food producers. Its members **campaign** for healthier practices in all areas of farming. They also campaign for better treatment of farm animals. The Soil Association encourages people to buy organic food from local farms.

Organic dairy farms

Cows on organic dairy farms feed on grass that has been grown without using chemicals. The cows are also fed some cereals, but these are chemical free. Organic farmers follow strict guidelines on what drugs they can use to treat sick cows.

Organic farmers claim that their dairy products are better for people's health.

Cruelty to hens?

Hens on factory farms are kept in very cramped conditions (see page 21). In recent years, some governments have recognized this fact and have made some moves to **ban** factory farming. The countries of the European Union have passed a law that all "factory" cages will be banned by 2012. They will be replaced by much larger cages with room for birds to perch and scratch on the floor. However, organizations such as Compassion in World Farming (see panel) say that hens should never be kept in cages.

Some egg farmers produce "barn eggs". These are not the same as free-range eggs, because the hens that produce them have to stay in huge sheds called percheries and cannot roam outside. About five per cent of eggs sold in the United Kingdom are "barn eggs".

Free-range hens

A growing number of farmers keep free-range hens. These hens are free to roam outside during the day. At night they sleep in barns with nesting boxes and perches.

Organic eggs

Organic eggs come from free-range hens that are fed entirely with organic food. During the day, the hens roam on land that has been farmed without the use of chemicals.

Today, over 45 per cent of eggs bought in the United Kingdom are "free-range".

Compassion in World Farming

Compassion in World Farming aims to stop all cruelty to animals on farms in the United Kingdom. Its members campaign peacefully against cruel practices such as keeping hens in "factory" cages, and zero grazing for dairy cows. Compassion in World Farming also gives prizes to farmers who treat their animals with compassion (kindness).

What's the future for dairy and egg production?

Many dairy farmers and egg producers choose to run very large-scale, intensive farms with the help of modern **technology**. Some farmers in the United States keep herds of over 15,000 cows. One American egg producer has a total of 26 million laying hens.

Going large

Most of the foods produced on large-scale farms are sold in supermarkets. But supermarkets are always trying to cut the price of food. This means the farmers are paid less for their products. Farmers today are under a lot of pressure to produce large quantities of food very cheaply.

Buying local

In some places, small-scale farmers avoid supermarkets completely. Instead, they run farm shops or sell their products at farmers' markets. Food that is sold at a farmers' market is more likely to be organic. But buyers should always ask the farmers about their practices. Many people are happy to spend more money when they buy from local farmers. They feel that they can trust the farmers to produce healthy food that does not involve any cruelty to animals.

Small and special

A growing number of dairy farmers and egg producers have decided to run small-scale farms. These farmers often use **organic farming** methods. Some small-scale dairy farmers make their own brands of cheese or yoghurt.

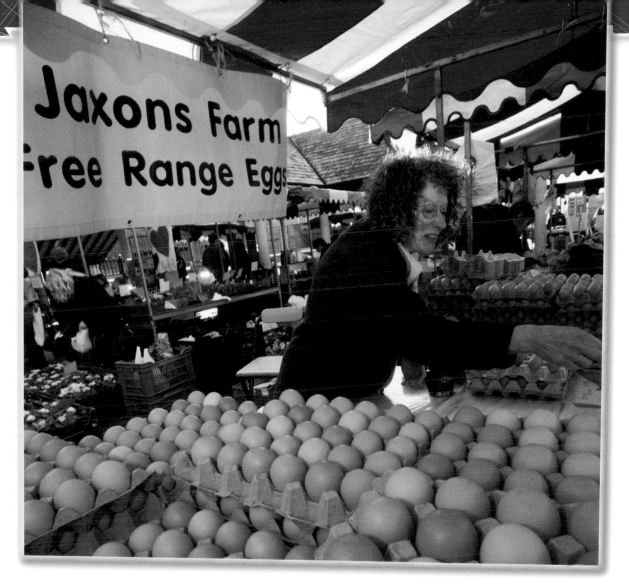

This farm has chosen to sell its free-range eggs at a farmers' market rather than a supermarket.

Future choices

Today's farmers face a difficult choice. Should they run a large-scale farm, using **intensive farming** methods to produce enormous quantities of food? Or should they concentrate on producing smaller amounts of high-quality food? High-quality food is expensive to produce, but it can be sold at a higher price.

Glossary

antibiotic drug that is used to cure infections

automatic happening without human control

bacteria tiny cells that are found in all living things. Some bacteria are useful, but others cause diseases.

ban to forbid something

campaign to take action in support of something

candling process of checking eggs by shining a light though them

centrifuge machine that spins liquids around very fast

conveyor belt moving belt that carries objects through a factory

curds solid part of fermented milk, when it separates into curds and whey

dairy products milk and other foods that are made from milk

developed country country that has many factories and uses high-level technology

factory farming type of farming where animals are kept in cages

fermented turned sour. When milk is turned into cheese, it is usually deliberately fermented by adding special bacteria to it.

fertilizer substance that is added to soil to make it richer

growth hormone drug that makes animals grow larger and stronger or produce more milk

high-protein very rich in protein. Proteins are needed by animals and humans to help their bodies grow and stay strong. High-protein foods help cows produce large amounts of milk.

homogenized processed so that the fat is spread evenly throughout a liquid

hygiene making sure that something is clean and free from germs

ingredient one of the items that is used to make a food

intensive farming farming that uses a lot of technology and chemicals in order to be as productive as possible

knead punch and stretch. Substances such as cheese curd and bread dough are kneaded to make them more elastic and springy.

mature to ripen and become stronger-tasting

milking parlour large building where cows are milked

organic farming farming that avoids all chemicals and aims to give farm animals a natural, healthy life

pasteurization heating milk to kill off some bacteria. Pasteurization makes milk last longer without turning sour, and it kills off some of the germs that spread diseases.

plant factory where dairy products or eggs are processed

polystyrene light, stiff plastic that is often used for packaging

processed treated and changed in some way. Milk is processed into butter and cheese.

productive able to produce more or make more

react to change in some way when mixed with another substance

rennet substance found in the stomach of cows that helps to separate milk into solid curds and liquid whey

roam to move around freely

robotic arm arm that is controlled by a computer

skimmed milk milk with almost all its fat removed

specialize concentrate on one skill

technology use of machinery and computers to do practical jobs

vaccination injection that prevents people from catching a disease

whey watery part of fermented milk, when it separates into curds and whey

zero grazing practice of keeping animals indoors and not allowing them to roam and eat outside

Find out more

Books

Farming in the Future (Food and Farming), Ian Graham
(Wayland, 2011)

Feeding the World (Food and Farming), Richard and Louise Spilsbury
(Wayland, 2011)

Food and Farming (Changes In...), Steve Parker (QED 2009)

Louis Pasteur and Pasteurization, Jennifer Fandel
(Raintree, 2011)

Sustainable Farming: How Can We Save Our World? Carol Ballard
(Franklin Watts, 2009)

Websites

This Is Dairy Farming

A website with lots of facts about UK dairy farming, including video
tours of a farm, and sections on "Caring for cows" and "Caring for
the environment".

www.dairyfarmingtoday.org/Pages/Home.aspx

British Lion Organization

The website of the British Lion Organization provides information on
all types of egg production.

www.egginfo.co.uk/page/eggproduction

The Soil Association

This website explains the aims of the Soil Association, and provides
information and news on organic farmers and farming practices. It also
has a list of organic farms in the United Kingdom that welcome visitors.

http://www.soilassociation.org

Compassion in World Farming (CIW)

This website explains the aims of CIW, and provides news of its campaigns against cruelty to farm animals.

www.ciwf.org.uk

Places to visit

Shugborough Hall, Staffordshire

Step back in time and visit a working Georgian farm at Shugborough Hall in Staffordshire. Watch dairymaids demonstrate 19th century methods of making butter and cheese, and see how the millwheel produces fine, wholmeal flour.

www.shugborough.org.uk/home-10

Museums

There are many local museums of rural life that give you a good idea of farming practices in the past. You can find your nearest museum by searching on the internet.

www.britainsfinest.co.uk/museums/search_results.cfm/searchclasscode/435

Farmers' markets

Use the website below to find a farmers' market near you. At many farmers' markets, you can talk to farmers who might be able to tell you more about their farming practices.

www.local-farmers-markets.co.uk

Agricultural shows

A great way to see farm animals and all the latest farm machinery is to visit an agricultural show. These shows often have livestock competitions and other agricultural events as well. Check on the internet to find a show near you that welcomes visitors.

Index